GREAT KITCHENS

JACK D. & OLETA NEITH

4880 Lower Valley Road, Atglen, Pennsylvania 19310

Schiffer Books are available at special discounts for bulk purchases for sales promotions or premiums. Special editions, including personalized covers, corporate imprints, and excerpts can be created in large quantities for special needs. For more information contact the publisher:

PUBLISHED BY Schiffer Publishing Ltd.
4880 Lower Valley Road
Atglen, PA 19310
Phone: (610) 593-1777; Fax: (610) 593-2002
E-mail: info@schifferbooks.com

For the largest selection of fine reference books on this and related subjects, please visit our web site at www.schifferbooks.com
We are always looking for people to write books on new and related subjects. If you have an idea for a book please contact us at the above address.

This book may be purchased from the publisher.
Include $3.95 for shipping.
Please try your bookstore first.
You may write for a free catalog.

IN EUROPE, Schiffer books are distributed by
Bushwood Books
6 Marksbury Ave.
Kew Gardens
Surrey TW9 4JF England
Phone: 44 (0) 20 8392-8585; Fax: 44 (0) 20 8392-9876
E-mail: info@bushwoodbooks.co.uk
Website: www.bushwoodbooks.co.uk
Free postage in the U.K., Europe; air mail at cost.

 COPYRIGHT © 2008 by Jack D. & Oleta Neith
Library of Congress Control Number: 2008922139

DESIGNED BY Laura Mikowychok. Type set in Zurich BT and Chapparal Pro.
ISBN: 978-0-7643-3008-7 | Printed in China

This book is dedicated to my husband Jack. Thank you for decades of love, understanding, and encouragement. This book exists because we traveled the world together and combined our talents, you as photographer and editor, and me as photo stylist, assistant, and author.

INTRODUCTION

Many people dream of having a beautiful kitchen, with state-of-the-art appliances, cabinets, and surfaces starring in an impeccably designed space. But when it comes to actually building such a kitchen, different tastes require different style choices, and different lifestyles require unique layouts for functionality and efficiency. With so many decisions to make, where does one begin?

This book features hundreds of kitchens in 330 images that speak to, excite, and inspire anyone who has wondered how their kitchen could run a little smoother, work a little harder, and be just a little bit more "them." The solutions shown in this book are for everyone, from the professional chef with only the finest tools, to the soccer mom who has just thirty minutes to create a meal for four, to the busy, single professional who can barely boil water. Not just square footage, or color scheme, but lifestyles truly determine what kitchen works best. A large, open floor plan with lots of seating works well for those who entertain frequently, and having two dishwashers, sinks, and refrigerators makes it easy to cook for a celebration. On the other hand, a modest-sized kitchen with a cozy table keeps family meals intimate. Meanwhile, a kitchen that includes a computer desk and an island with breakfast bar serves the on-the-go lifestyle of today's multi-tasking parent, student, or business professional. But function isn't everything; kitchens take beautiful forms when done well, making the spaces as pleasant to inhabit as they are simple to use. Contemporary, country, European, Art Deco, traditional, and retro styles are all illustrated here in a variety of arrangements, showing how colors, textures, and surface materials all contribute to the best kitchen for you and your family.

Photographed exclusively by Jack D. Neith in homes across the United States, these images illustrate how to solve storage problems, choose color schemes that make a room look bigger, and help you decide what floor plan and materials you like best. Armed with these professional, full-color photographs, homeowners can discuss design options with their interior designers feeling educated and prepared. This book is sure to inspire a fun remodeling of your existing kitchen, or help you decide what direction to take when designing a new kitchen. Either way, knowing the possibilities for your dream kitchen is the first step to making it a reality.

FOR THIS KITCHEN, see page 36. ▸

Beauty and function work harmoniously in this expansive kitchen with traditional flare. Granite countertops adorn exquisite custom cabinets, and a multi-purpose island contains a state-of-the-art cook top. Two ceiling fans add comfort and stylishly blend in with inviting décor. Entertaining is fun and easy with lots of countertop space and an open floor plan.

INSET: Detail of the corner cabinet reveals built-in turntables that provide convenient storage of spices, herbs, and condiments. The appliance garage below decoratively houses small appliances behind a rolling tambour door. Detailed cabinet borders are expertly honed to look like rope, and doorknobs complement with a matching shape in silvery knotted metal.

A sweeping open floor plan with wide aisles creates easy movement between the island and the perimeter wall cabinets in this custom space. Muted terra cotta hues in floor tiles anchor the collection of earth tones. The professional series refrigerator covered in wood panels blends perfectly with the cabinets to form an unbroken finish. High ceilings add to the overall feeling of unobstructed space.

Cerise chair cushions create a subtle contrast to the green glass table top and the greenery viewed through the glass double doors. A ceiling fan provides additional comfort. Tantalizing outdoor vistas bring the beauty of nature inside through the old world charm of patio doors and the windows behind the sink. Every meal is a treat in this luxurious kitchen.

OPPOSITE: Strategically placed, a wine rack in the island backs up to the bar area to create a convenient work station. The island also features a multitude of storage spaces, a convenient stovetop, and casual dining for two. Warm, rich earth tones complement the beige backdrop created by the floor tiles, walls, and ceiling. The separate bar area with a sink and wine cooler is the ultimate convenience in this kitchen.

INSET: A glass-front cabinet door reveals priceless crystal as decorative art adorns the wall and countertop. This nook is perfect for preparing cocktails for two or beverages for a large crowd. The backsplash is covered with detailed terra cotta tile with a complementary bas-relief design. The gourmet garage has a tambour door front and elegantly houses small appliances in easy reach.

The decorative ceiling cove is boldly colored in a floral pattern with a red-orange background, rich green leaves, and delicate white flowers. This delightful design element houses a fan suspended over the seating area. The natural concrete table base is a Tuscan inspired urn, on display through the glass tabletop.

1 & 2 Wall murals are artfully painted in subtle earth hues and soft brush strokes. The artist took great care duplicating the hues of cabinets and countertops, to match the actual kitchen. Even the door handles are painted in exact and precise detail.

1

2

Honey hues and warm beiges contrast majestically with stainless steel appliances in this contemporary kitchen. The angled counter peninsula gives movement and visual interest to the design. Cooking space turns into dining space for two on the peninsula of drawers and shelves that create storage space and a display of chinaware. A tall wall cabinet serves as an anchor with transparent glass doors that reveal dishes and stemware. Complementary artwork hangs above the dining area in warm earth tones depicting a pleasing landscape with flourishes of blue and green.

1 The sink is strategically placed in front of a lovely bowed window that provides luxuriant natural light. Under-mount double bowls make this sink timeless in design and convenient in form and function. The overall design is further enhanced with cabinet hardware in polished steel and a decorative patterned tile back splash in steel gray.

1

2

2 Wall tiles in beige and gray complement the warm honey tones of the cabinets and wood floor while coordinating with the gray granite counter tops and stainless steel appliances. The range hood adds to the sleek, contemporary design of the kitchen with clean, elegant lines in stainless steel. Double doors open conveniently to the backyard porch. High beige ceilings and neutral walls, doors and window trims form the perfect backdrop for a spacious feeling within a modest-sized room.

A large island takes center stage in this elegant, traditional kitchen. A stainless steel sink, stovetop, and ample storage are all gloriously housed within its confines. Warm beige cabinets complement the beige and white of ceiling, walls, columns, and dining chairs. Covered in glossy black and gray granite, this island commands attention with eye opening details and remarkable depth of color. The open floor plan allows easy access to the family room, creating a warm invitation to travel between the spaces.

INSET: This countertop detail shows the remarkable depth of color and interest within the granite. Neutral ceiling moldings, columns, and chandelier create an eegant and formal kitchen. These neutral shades with high ceilings create a spacious room.

Elegant beige leather chairs enhance the formal setting of this neutral kitchen with beige walls, ceiling, floor, and cabinets. A glass tabletop mirrors the shape of the island, stabilizing the design. The range hood is made of rough, rustic, irregular stones in tan, gray, and taupe hues. A handy, leather-covered stool provides seating at the island for a quick snack or casual meal.

INSET: Double wall ovens and a microwave are conveniently located behind the stovetop, and an additional sink provides ample workspace beneath a window to the right.

The smooth, shiny surface of the granite countertops contrast elegantly with a warm wood floor and pristine cabinetry. A unique oval window in the butler's pantry resembles the fine lines and details of a spider web. Creative and innovative design details are further enhanced by lead glass window designs throughout the kitchen. The island has many fine details including hanging baskets below to store cooking staples such as potatoes and onions, a built-in towel rack, and finely crafted sculptural columns and bas-relief scrolls.

INSET: Glistening natural light dances through numerous windows with lead glass ornamentation. Decorative and functional columns anchor the custom cabinetry in warm white. The warm neutrals of a high ceiling create an inviting culinary retreat, while seemingly endless countertops provide a multitude of cooking space and elegantly display flowers, plants, and chinaware.

Decorative carvings embellish wood-work around a professional stove, which includes eight surface burners and two large ovens below. This is truly a gourmet delight that enables easy food preparation for a large party. Beige stone tiles create a subtle and decorative backsplash. Columnar cabinets on either side of the stove are highly decorative and fully functional with tiny, doored compartments for herbs, spices, and other essentials.

The capacious center island is equipped with a deep, round sink and is lit with an elegant chandelier of copper with glowing amber glass. Unique in form, yet complementary in color and materials, another light fixture illuminates the seating area to the right. Floor-to-ceiling windows encompass the back door.

ABOVE: This moderately sized kitchen provides comfort with a clean, modern design featuring light hues. Earthenware vessels and potted green plants enhance an earthy color palette. The spacious countertop doubles as dining space with ample room to seat four comfortably. Multi-paned double doors provide privacy from the rest of the house.

RIGHT: Glass-paned double doors between the kitchen and family rooms allow privacy when desired. Entertaining with the doors open connects the two rooms for better guest interaction. Appliances blend into the woodwork with matching cabinet panels as long countertops supply ample surfaces for food preparation and decorative display.

Contemporary elegance abounds in this masterfully designed kitchen. Bright accent bowls, flowers, and fruits and vegetables add excitement and flair to the dramatic dark tones of Italian granite countertops. A moderate space benefits from a cook top on the island and seating for three along the peninsula of cabinets. Luxurious, dark, earthen hues of the floor tiles anchor this sensational design.

INSET: A comfortable, open floor plan progresses from the kitchen through the rest of the house. Large floor-to-ceiling windows allow glistening natural light to dance upon the shiny surfaces and fill the entire room with life. Neutral wall colors extend from the kitchen through the family room for a cohesive design that accentuates a spacious feeling. Complementary floor and wall tiles solidify the unity of earth tones.

Rich, dark wood cabinets contrast well with neutral walls, floor, and ceiling. Floral accents on the chairs, window treatment, and wall border add a homey touch. A solid surface countertop on the island provides elegance and a splash of green color with white trim that goes nicely with the countertop backsplash and window curtain. An assortment of tools dangles conveniently from the rack above the stove. Three can dine at the island while sitting on chairs of a delicate floral tapestry. Cooking and cleaning is quick and easy with a solid surface under-mount sink with two deep bowls and self-contained drain board on the right. Large windows provide natural light and a lovely view for those tending to tasks at the sink.

ABOVE: Dramatic lighting and rich wood cabinetry produces a strong statement in this country-style kitchen. Modern appliances and custom cabinets create a chef's delight in a renovated older home. The large angular window behind the sink stretches from the countertop to the ceiling, showing tantalizing views of the scenic gardens outside. Glass-front cabinet doors reveal treasures on display while creating the illusion of more windows.

RIGHT: Gleaming granite countertops supply a handy work station and comfortable eating area atop this rectangular island. The cook top is conveniently located to the side of the refrigerator and wall ovens, behind the sink. Honey-kissed hardwood floors complement the richly hued cabinets, tying the design together.

Romantic ambiance abounds in this kitchen of rich, dark hues. Polished, forest green solid surface countertops create contrasts against colorful foods and culinary decorations. **INSET:** Exquisite workmanship in cabinetry design is shown in this burgundy and hunter green cabinet. Glass-front drawer cabinets store dried beans and pasta, and an open plate rack above is both colorful and convenient.

This detail shows a decorative cabinet area that is used as a bar as well as a pass-through to the adjacent dining room. Glistening crystal stemware hangs elegantly above the counter in this custom glass rack. Transparent glass-front cabinet doors provide shimmering views of the china within.

1 Detailed craftsmanship is apparent in a columnar design that enhances the corner edge of the base cabinetry. Rich wood grain blends with this timeless kitchen design.

2 Baseboard heating elements are creatively disguised with delicate carved wood accents.

LEFT: Light and bright, this kitchen has a cottage-by-the-sea feeling. Crisp white cabinets are contrasted by blue window treatments and china. The curving edge of the island seats four comfortably and creates delightful movement within the space. White wooden stools with natural cane seats solidify a homey feel. A marriage of contemporary stainless steel and timeless green sea glass forms the stove hood.

BELOW: The center island not only provides comfortable seating, it houses a dishwasher and a large sink. In addition, there is ample storage below and countertop space above. Colors, textures, and surfaces contrast harmoniously within this kitchen. A solid surface white countertop above white cabinets contrasts with warm brown hues of island cabinets topped with smooth, lacquered granite. Light brown hues of the hardwood floor blend beautifully with the island cabinets. Cutouts in the wall cabinets are decorative and functional as they house books, china, and culinary accoutrements at an arm's reach.

1

Curving walls and tall ceilings amplify spaciousness in this fashionable kitchen. Floor-to-ceiling cabinets of hard maple surround the room and provide ample storage for the serious cook. Whether cooking for two or twenty, the large triangular floor plan is great for cooking and comfortable for mingling. Colorful flowers, accessories, food, and green plants complement a natural palette of earth tones. A professional range and double wall ovens provide the ultimate in cooking convenience.

1 Gourmet dinners or casual snacks are enjoyed at the triangular center island with three cozy seats. Professional-grade tools and dried peppers dangle from a steel rack. The island sink is great for a quick clean up; a side wine rack houses a handy selection of spirits. The polished range hood has a shelf below, perfect for spices and flavorings. The seat cushions, rug, and window treatment add a touch of complementary patterns.

2 Paisley window treatments in festive hues of orange, peach, and blue enliven the view to a lush, green outdoors. The wall covering above the cabinets complements the curtains with like colors and similar shapes.

2

Neutral white walls, floor, and ceiling are the perfect backdrop for a stylish, modern kitchen that feels warm and welcoming. Mottled tan and brown granite covers a long expanse of rich cherry cabinets. Visual interest continues with the use of two tones of cherry. Natural light glistens atop the gleaming granite, making food prep a pleasure. A built-in bench produces an intimate dining area conveniently located within the kitchen.

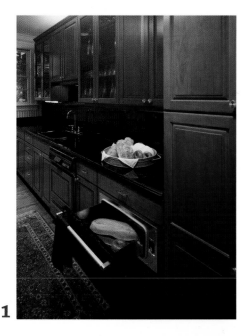

1

2

3

The large butler's pantry is exquisitely equipped with custom cabinets in warm wood tones with complementary countertops in the finest ebony granite. Glass paned doors on the wall cabinets cleanly display crystal stemware and heirloom china. A long stretch of countertop allows for easy food preparation for both large parties and intimate meals. The gray-and-white-striped wall adds ocular interest as the high white ceiling and large window create a feeling of open space.

1 Top-of-the-line appliances adorn the butler's pantry and blend in with the cabinets. The stove features a convenient warming tray to keep fresh-baked breads warm and ready for the dining table.

2 Decorative hand-blown glass vases in bright red, orange, and blue are stored safely and elegantly with crystal stemware in a pantry wall cabinet.

3 Majestic ivory marble with ebony and gray veins makes a beautiful ornamental statement around an arched doorway. A formal butler's pantry is visible through the open door, revealing detailed custom cabinets and a black granite counter. An Oriental carpet graces the medium brown hardwood floor, providing comfort and design interest.

Traditional charm surrounds you as you enter this inviting kitchen. Warm, rich wood tones of cabinets are complemented by light hues in shiny granite countertops. A bold mosaic of navy blue and buttercup yellow tiles above the stovetop catches the eye. A blue refrigerator cabinet intensifies a colorful kitchen scheme and ties in with a blue inlaid floor design and tiled backsplash.

1 An extension of the counter area provides intimate dining for two with a beautiful on durable granite in swirling tones of taupe, beige, and brown.

2 This butler's pantry has lovely honey-hued wooden cabinets covered in hardwood butcher-block, eliminating the need for extra cutting boards. Beige walls and ceiling coax a spacious feeling from a narrow area.

1

2

The professional series stove is enhanced by the convenience of a pot-filling water faucet. No need to lug a heavy pot of water from the sink to the stove; just place your pot on the range, drop in your vegetables or pasta, and fill. A dramatic country blue cabinet discreetly houses a refrigerator with lower drawer freezer.

Lily-white cabinets encompass this kitchen with glowing country charm. Lustrous ebony granite bedecks the base cabinets with tasteful opulence and strong color contrast. The island includes a third sink, multiple storage drawers, a microwave oven, and a large countertop surface for food preparation and service. A custom wine rack above the secondary sink adds charm, and glistening stemware dangles neatly in a row beneath. A traditional baker's rack in white wrought iron ties in country allure with visual enticement and functional flair.

INSET: Gleaming glass window panes make a strong visual statement on wall cabinets surrounding the stove in this kitchen. The entire wall shimmers with ocular delight as these doors stretch from counter to ceiling. High ceilings and predominantly white hues embellish and enhance the spaciousness to new heights, while cozy hardwood floors ground the room. The professional stove is fully equipped with warming baskets below the hood.

A Southwest theme permeates in this modern kitchen with terracotta accents in floor tiles, decorative china, and earthenware. Creamy cabinets with dark metal hardware tie in with a smooth, dark tabletop, stove front, and dishwasher. Cane-backed chairs in an ebony and ivory weave are the finishing touch. Luscious green succulents in terracotta pots adorn the table and counters, bringing a piece of the desert indoors. The curvature of cabinets creates a great work space and adds movement to the space. Solid surface countertops in moderate gray complement the design and do not distract from the warm earth tones.

Warm, white cabinets pop with traditional charm in this extravagant kitchen. Elegantly displayed culinary accessories are a tantalizing delight in every nook and cranny. Potted flowers and herbs bask in natural light from countertop-to-ceiling windows. The cabinet behind the island recalls the grace and charm of Hoosier cabinets of yesteryear.

1 Traditional elegance commingles with modern technology in a center island equipped with a solid surface cook top – a joy to use and easy to keep clean. Warm yellow walls embrace the room and complement the honey hues of wood and earth tones in granite surfaces.

2 A curving archway reveals a view of a handsomely shelved wall unit. Unique canisters in the shapes of houses are proudly displayed with other family heirlooms. Floor-to-ceiling wall units encompass the adjoining hall with a romantic, secluded bench seat beneath the window. Warm, white cabinets, wainscot below the window, and matching yellow fabric for the seat cushion and window treatment work to achieve continuity. Warm tones of hardwood anchor the cozy feeling throughout the kitchen and hallway.

1

Honey hues of walls, floor, countertops, and accessories produce a cozy feeling in this kitchen. Double wall ovens make preparing meals for parties quick and easy. Glass-front doors on upper cabinets work with high ceilings and light color schemes to create a truly open kitchen. Under foot, a tapestry carpet adds warmth and interesting texture.

INSET: A curving archway reveals a view of a handsomely shelved wall unit. Unique canisters in the shapes of houses are proudly displayed with other family heirlooms. Floor-to-ceiling wall units encompass the adjoining hall with a romantic, secluded bench seat beneath the window. Warm, white cabinets, wainscot below the window, and matching yellow fabric for the seat cushion and window treatment work to achieve continuity. Warm tones of hardwood anchor the cozy feeling throughout the kitchen and hallway.

NEXT PAGE: "Quaint and charming" describes this country kitchen of crisp white walls and brilliant blue accents. Festive window treatments in canary yellow and dusty blue enhance light as it passes through large windows in the sink and dining areas. Hardwood floors complement maple cabinets with blue accents. The island accommodates seating for two and has ample storage, including three shelves displaying vintage canning jars, plants, and baskets.

1 This kitchen is full of specialty cabinets, including the opened cabinet next to the refrigerator. Sliding doors slip into side pockets, opening up the work area for a mixer and blender. Above the island, sparkling copper pots and pans hang from a custom rack made of the cabinets' hard maple.

2 A desk creates a splendid contemporary workstation. Practical shelves above provide storage for cookbooks. Interior cabinets and shelves painted Colonial blue add country charm, and tie in the decorative wall border.

3 A detailed dish rack allows easy access to china, with drawers underneath to accommodate silverware and cloth napkins. Colonial blue glass-front doors expose a collection of vintage teapots.

1

Floor-to-cathedral-ceiling windows create an extraordinary backdrop for this avant-garde kitchen. Gleaming white cabinets, ceiling and walls command attention amidst the vast open space. The beige tile floor is accented with small black tiles in a contemporary diamond inlaid design. The sink beneath a great wall of luminescent windows appears to float above the surface of the floor. Modern cabinets throughout the kitchen are equipped with state-of-the-art ingenuity, like a wood cutting board that slides out from under the countertop, and a built-in desk beneath a picturesque window readies the kitchen for multitasking.

1

2

3

Towering at great heights, a larger-than-life image of Picasso's nude is executed in glistening blue and white ceramic tiles. Bold and provocative, this mural commands center stage. The natural wood tone of the sink cabinet reflects the beauty of nature's picturesque trees in dazzling sunlight.

1 A handy board extension slides out from under the countertop for extra space to set pots, pans, and other cooking tools between the stove and wall ovens. This kitchen is equipped with many professional amenities, including a built-in deep-frying unit.

2 This base cabinet provides functional and easy storage for heavy appliances such as stand mixers and food processors. Appliances are housed out of view when not needed and are easy to access when needed, perched atop individual boards that pull up and out. The boards can be set at different levels to accommodate chefs who are tall, average, or short in height.

3 An elegant cabinet with frosted glass window fronts provides ample space to store a variety of crystal stemware. Preparing cocktails for family and guests is expedient and fun with a spacious counter on which to place glasses, serving vessels, spirits, and ice while allowing for lemon and lime slicing, too. The sink is the icing on the cake for the ultimate in bartending.

Bluish-gray walls between the countertop and wall cabinets produce an air of serenity in this large kitchen. Glass-front doors on all of the wall cabinets contribute to an open feeling in this space. Warm white ceiling and light fixtures solidify a clean, contemporary environment. Contemporary cabinets are embraced with Southwestern charm within this delightful kitchen. A combination of rich, peach hues of the cabinets and complementary blue tones of the countertop and the wall creates visual impact. Checkerboard tiles in gray and bone add a colorful touch to the floor in this inviting space.

Creative contrast is established between the shiny, ebony, granite island countertop and the dull finish of a blue composite countertop to the left. A checkered tile floor leads to the dining table with woven cane chairs. The table is illuminated with a contemporary ceiling-hung light fixture. This picturesque view leads through to the living room with a fireplace of colorful and textured fieldstone.

INSET: The center island is a chef's delight with a sleek ebony granite countertop and lots of storage space. Most of the custom base cabinets in this kitchen are equipped with sturdy, pullout shelves like this one, for pots, pans, and assorted bake ware. The handy cabinet at the far end of the island is a great hideaway for waste disposal.

1

2

3

Bright white elements create a clean, contemporary design in this kitchen. White cabinets glisten with light from a rectangular skylight above. Frosty blue walls add a touch of color while keeping the mood cool and crisp. A modernistic, built-in wine rack with circular openings holds bottles neatly. The space is moderately sized, yet spacious in feel due to high ceilings, light colors, and natural light.

1 Smooth, sleek cabinet surfaces camouflage the refrigerator and produce a polished, contemporary feel. Rounded edges of cabinets and countertops accentuate the contemporary design. A glass-front cabinet door reveals elegant groupings of chinaware.

2 A double bowl sink complements with brilliant white color and deep bowls, equipped with a handy hot water dispenser, soap pump, and faucet with removable head. A built-in corner shelf behind the sink provides added space to display a plant or cooking décor.

3 A streamlined countertop is fashioned in durable solid surface material used as the tabletop as well. Elegant dining is achieved within this borders of this spacious, contemporary kitchen. White appliances melt into the background and floor-to-ceiling cabinets supply ample storage.

White cabinets are covered with gray solid surface countertops for an elegant design. Hidden storage space is reclaimed with a triangular shelf next to the refrigerator. Natural wood butcher-block covers the stovetop counter, and provides relaxed dining for two.

INSET: The stovetop peninsula in this kitchen overlooks the dining table in the adjacent room, keeping the chef connected to guests. Muted green walls with burgundy accents create an inviting dining area with a contemporary flair.

1

2

Mosaic floor tiles in pink, red, black, and white that border the cabinets are jovial as confetti. The tiled backsplash complements the floor design with a structured pattern of color and shape. The combination of white surfaces and textures with high ceilings and a skylight help make this small kitchen appear large and inviting.

1 Crisp white cabinets come to life with a vivid red countertop, and white walls and ceiling provide a neutral backdrop. Tantalizing sunlight filters through the glass paned door, windows, and skylight.

2 With a stovetop conveniently located next to the wall ovens, the task of cooking is an enjoyable one. The stepped wall behind the counter features tile accents that create a visual separation between the kitchen and the dining area. A spice rack is neatly spaced between shelves for book and condiment storage, all conveniently close to the oven and range. Small appliances are neatly stored behind a tambour door beneath the shelves.

Floor to ceiling columns contribute to formal elegance in this dynamic kitchen. The island sports a second sink, perfect for washing garden-fresh vegetables. There is plenty of room for food preparation on top, and ample storage space below.

INSET The angular design of custom cabinets creates movement and interest in this kitchen of traditional details and strong color, shape, and surface contrasts. Bright whites of the walls, ceiling, floor tiles, and solid surface countertops contrast elegantly with the dark hue of the cabinets. Sunlight dances through the glass panes of floor-to-ceiling windows in the adjacent dining room, as well as through the beveled windows behind the sink, enhancing the spaciousness of this striking design.

Contrasting red and green accents brighten this spacious black and white traditional kitchen. Crisp white cabinets, major appliances, walls, and ceiling create a clean environment. Beaming sunlight filters through six large windows with serene landscape views in tantalizing greens and earth tones. Gleaming black granite countertops encircle the entire kitchen with vast amounts of space for food preparation and homey decorations like vivid purple violets in individual ceramic pots.

INSET: This long, rectangular island has a conveniently located stove top, the refrigerator and double wall ovens placed directly behind it. The expansive countertop has more than enough room to roll out pastry or pasta dough for a delicious apple pie, a batch of homemade pierogies, or a fresh lasagna.

Warm beige tiles adorn the floor and decorate the wall behind the stove top, complementing the neutral ceiling and walls. Major appliances blend into the woodwork with custom wood fronts that match the cabinets. **INSET:** Deep brown cabinets are suspended above ebony granite countertops in this stylish kitchen. An angular island creates interesting movement within the curving space. Two dine comfortably at an island that boasts a secondary sink and numerous drawers and cabinets for storage. A curvaceous window above the sink relinquishes a breathtaking view of backyard trees and shrubs in forest greens.

Magnificent red cherry cabinets take center stage in this elegant kitchen. Informal dining for three at the kitchen counter is convenient and comfortable. Beige floor tiles and wall coverings form a pleasant, neutral backdrop for the entire scene.

A sea of dazzling white cabinets surround this huge kitchen. Light hardwood floors anchor the design with the help of dark floor tiles circling the massive island. A multitude of storage space is available in the island, including glass-front doors that elegantly expose glass shelves with ornate accoutrements.

1

2

A deep sink of the same material as the solid surface countertop creates a seamless flow of surfaces and textures below the window in a striking semicircle design. Beautiful cut flowers and potted flowering plants bring the beauty of nature indoors, enhancing the picturesque view through the window.

1 Romantic dining for two is strategically set within the comfort of the kitchen. Delicate wall covering adds a touch of color to the otherwise pristine, white environment. Elegant white candles in white candlestick holders complete this lovely monochromatic setting.

2 A shiny black stovetop is neatly nestled between a microwave oven above and a conventional oven below. Symmetry continues within this kitchen design with the wall cabinets surrounding the microwave oven, which provide comfort and ease to the chef.

1 Muted green cabinets within a sea of beige give a tropical air to this contemporary kitchen. The round window above the neutral sink is artfully embellished with a pink floral design. The freestanding wall cabinet above the stovetop provides convenient storage for spices.

2 The island houses ample storage space in addition to accommodating a dishwasher conveniently located behind the sink for quick and easy clean-up. Baking for the holidays and large parties is easy with double wall ovens.

3 Tropical flare continues into the adjacent dining area with lush green foliage and complementary artwork. Symmetrical windows behind the table add a touch of formality to the laid-back comfort of this space. Warm beige floor tiles, countertops, walls, and ceiling surfaces make this space appear larger than it actually is.

1

2

3

The stainless steel refrigerator and sleek design of a stainless steel stove hood further enhance this kitchen's clean, dramatic lines. Exquisite granite perpetuates the seamless flow of extraordinary colors. Tall ceilings and an open floor plan create a spacious environment. Functional elements, tantalizing textures, and comfort with flair create an inviting gathering spot for everyone that enters.

INSET: The contemporary elements of hard maple cabinets and wall ovens form a clean, sleek interior design with expansive surrounding storage, providing easy kitchen organization. The built-in desk provides access to a computer, while the cabinet above allows tidy storage embellished with frosted glass doors.

OPPOSITE: Muted hues of rust, bluish-gray and taupe swirl seamlessly along a flowing countertop of gleaming granite atop hard maple cabinets. Elegant seating for four surrounds the rounded counter that loops to form a delightful eating area. Beige, natural Italian floor tiles set on an angle graciously complement the light brown cabinets and warm beige walls. The wall of windows above the sink and on the other side of the curved counter wall brings inside the beauty of the outdoors.

An accent wall of textured brick creates an enhanced cottage feeling against cheerful white. This wall encases the ovens as well as storage cabinets. The island has a contrasting countertop in charcoal gray and seats two. Additional storage space and the cook top are also in the island, providing the ultimate in function. The neutral hues and metallic accents of various chinaware, cooking utensils, and decorative items complement the color scheme.

INSET: Black and white tiles form a diamond pattern on the floor that complements the overall design of this French-cottage-inspired kitchen. Brown cabinets add warmth and depth to a predominately white and ebony color scheme. The walls are covered in a delightful Toile du Juoy pastoral scene in black on a cream background. The kitchen is surrounded with an abundance of windows, allowing serene vistas of nature's actual pastoral beauty to infiltrate the room.

A pleasing blend of patterns, colors, and surfaces produce an inviting feeling in this kitchen. Toile du Juoy window treatments and wall coverings have a pleasing pattern repeated in black on a cream field. The plaid wall covering adds brown to the ivory and black, tying in the color elements of the cabinetry. A simple chandelier hangs above a romantic table for two with bluish-gray chair and door detail, complementing the hue of the island countertop.

INSET: The sink is visually enhanced by a large window with peaceful landscape views. Toile du Juoy covers the wall in this formal, yet cozy kitchen. The long, white, solid surface countertop ensures ample space for food preparation and blends pleasingly with the white sink, wall tiles, and white woodwork surrounding the windows.

Stainless steel professional appliances and shiny black granite countertops elegantly complement the rich brown hues of the cabinets in this timeless kitchen. The island workstation is a true chef's delight with a secondary sink, ample storage space, and seating for two. INSET: The gentle curve of this kitchen provides a comfortable work flow and gives the room elegant grace. Light brown floor tiles tie in natural earth tones of wall coverings, cabinets, and ceiling for a very unified look.

Contrasting textures produce visual focal points as the black and white countertop, stove, and wall tiles pop from the rich cherry of surrounding cabinets and hardwood flooring. A matching cherry door front covers a built-in refrigerator, which appears as just another cabinet.

INSET: A built-in desk completes the comfort and practicality of this extravagant kitchen. A beautifully detailed wall cabinet above the desk has many nooks and crannies to accommodate an array of computer and stationery supplies.

Deep-hued cabinets of brilliant cherry form this hyoid design. Shiny white wall tiles make a pleasing backdrop as they complement white solid surface countertops. The under mount sink is of the same material as the counter and serves well with a large, deep bowl. Pink and red cyclamens bloom happily amidst the sparkling sunlight in a custom window outcropping where glowing natural light streams in from above and around simultaneously.

INSET: Intricate tile design adds contrast and drama to a kitchen wall. Smooth, shiny tile surfaces complement the counter and stovetop, while contrasting with the warm, deep hues of wood cabinets.

A splash of color from the area rug beneath the sink adds pleasing texture and added comfort to this space. Large windows nurture the potted rose on the countertop beneath.

Warm beige and taupe surfaces and textures encapsulate this luxurious, expansive kitchen. Contemporary stainless steel wall ovens complement the elegant, traditional décor. Auburn flooring produces stability within this environment of floating neutral tones. The uniquely shaped island can easily accommodate seating for four if desired. Mottled earth tone hues in the gleaming granite countertop create formal elegance and provide long expanses of workspace. Three large windows above the sink permit swaths of natural sunlight to bathe the space with luminance, thus exaggerating the open feeling in the kitchen.

INSET: Decorative china pieces are elegantly displayed on shelves within the island, which are exquisitely embellished with bas relief scroll designs in matching wood. A microwave oven is conveniently housed within the island below the sink, adding yet another convenience.

Floor to ceiling cabinets provide lots of storage space with transparent window panes throughout. This part of the kitchen is formally bordered by white columns and framed with a decorative wall covering of autumn colored leaves and flowers on a complementary taupe field.

The combination of angles and curves in the cabinet design produce visual interest in the movement and floor space in the kitchen. The large island has two levels of countertop. The lower level is a long, angular area for food preparation. The upper level is decoratively curved which is not only beautiful to look at, but adds a convenient table surface with the addition of chairs. Ample storage in numerous drawers and shelves complete the island. A professional stove is majestically surrounded with luxurious textures, hues, and surfaces. The tile wall is complementary with light cream tiles and dark tiles mottled with taupe and beige. Intricate sculptural accents in bas-relief embellish the stove hood. Symmetrical cabinet design around the stove produces a formal, anchored design.

Majestic columns in a faux marble finish frame this view of a striking contemporary kitchen and adjacent dining room. Glistening Italian marble floors and a faux marble finish on the walls enhance a regal design. Cool neutral tones add to the formal setting while high ceilings create an open environment. Dramatic lighting enhances visual ambiance and lures visitors inside with beauty and extravagance.

Modern white cabinets cover every inch of this incredible kitchen. Gleaming ebony granite with speckles of white top the island and form a curving tabletop with dining for two. Bright white ceiling and floor surfaces complete the envelope of monochromatic splendor. Friends and family gather comfortably in this spacious, contemporary kitchen.

1 The island is equipped with a state-of-the-art stovetop in deep ebony. An assortment of culinary accoutrements of shiny copper and sparkling stainless steel hangs within easy reach from the steel rack above the stove. The fluidity of white light continues with white ovens and the white, cabinet-paneled dishwasher.

2 This kitchen comes complete with an expansive desk area conveniently built into the cabinetry. Glass windowpanes adorn two cabinets on either side of the desk in this symmetrical design; nooks and crannies of various sizes and shapes provide elegant display areas for cherished accessories as well as ample space to store stationery supplies.

PREVIOUS: To say that this kitchen is "enormous" would be a veritable understatement. Clearly one of the largest kitchens in this book, it is filled with an endless array of culinary delights. Color plays an important role in the exquisite design; there is a delicate balance of the contrasting and the complementary. The open floor plan of this room exaggerates the expansive actual square footage. Warm brown hues of the dining table blend flawlessly with the hardwood floors. Priceless Oriental carpets create visual boundaries within the space and anchor the long rectangular table that accommodates eight in cozy culinary comfort. Deep royal blue covers the far wall while sea foam green adorns the wall beyond the island. These tranquil colors paint an inviting backdrop in a voluminous kitchen filled with inspiring and welcoming features.

This kitchen boasts two distinct islands with unique elements in each. The island in the foreground provides an elegant and private writing desk as well as a convenient sink. The long rectangular island in the background includes a stovetop and comfortable seating for four. Both provide vast amounts of storage space. There is a subtle contrast in color between island cabinets in honey brown hues, and kitchen cabinets in warm, creamy light beiges. Nature's outdoor beauty is visible through the spacious Venetian windows surrounded by cool green walls. Cathedral ceilings of white seem to float above the entire space. Contrast in textures is evident between the multicolored rough surface of fieldstones forming the fireplace and the smooth light surfaces that surround it. Elegant at every turn, this kitchen is a true delight.

1

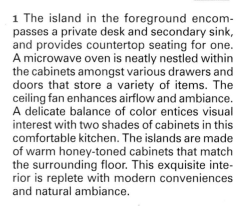

2

1 The island in the foreground encompasses a private desk and secondary sink, and provides countertop seating for one. A microwave oven is neatly nestled within the cabinets amongst various drawers and doors that store a variety of items. The ceiling fan enhances airflow and ambiance. A delicate balance of color entices visual interest with two shades of cabinets in this comfortable kitchen. The islands are made of warm honey-toned cabinets that match the surrounding floor. This exquisite interior is replete with modern conveniences and natural ambiance.

2 The entire length of the back wall accommodates a complete bar with sink, dishwasher, and under counter refrigerator. An intricate tile mosaic decorates the wall behind the sink in rich, vibrant colors. Specialty shelves include an ornate wine rack and gleaming glass door fronts on all of the upper wall cabinets. Sparkling crystal is displayed elegantly in this symmetrical design. Beige wall tiles complement the light cabinets and encourage a spacious feeling. Turquoise walls create a vivid separation of color between the white ceiling and beige cabinets for a unique visual frame.

1 Large niches above the cabinets contain decorative still-life groupings of pottery in terracotta, turquoise, white, and tan. One pot contains a flowering plant with vibrant red flowers, and another holds a desert succulent with lush foliage, for a Southwestern feeling with local plants and touches of American Indian pottery.

2 Cool white walls and ceiling reflect natural sunlight through the Palladian window and two skylights. Creamy cabinets complement the neutral hue of the floor tiles, walls, and ceiling. The island seats two for casual meals, and contains a wine rack for twenty-four bottles. Bright pitchers, bowls, and other accoutrements in blues, reds, yellows, and greens add a delightfully fun palette to a backdrop of neutral tones.

2

1

3 The island countertop combines a mottled granite surface with specks of browns, blacks, and beiges. The secondary sink and numerous drawers for storage enhance its usefulness. Large, rectangular wall openings between the kitchen and adjoining rooms create vistas common in traditional desert dwellings.

3

1 Country charm fills this beautiful and inviting kitchen. Light blond wood cabinets reflect the warm glow of natural and artificial light sources. The island contains additional counter space for food preparation with a stovetop, shelves, and drawers for storing condiments and other culinary needs. Warm colors and a welcoming design create a cozy and comfortable gathering place for family and friends. The round dining table and chairs match the wood cabinets impeccably and provide intimate dining for four with an incredible view of nature's splendor beyond the double glass doors.

2 Beneath the kitchen window, fresh herbs grow in ample sunlight during daytime hours. The double bowl sink is large and deep, making food preparation and clean up tasks easy. A pleasing checkered design is created in beige and terracotta tiles on the wall complementing the cabinets, countertop, and walls. A delightful farm scene adorns the niche above the window, adding a delicate and homey touch to the country charm in this kitchen.

1

3

2

3 The adjacent dining area is set apart with an accent wall of decorative plaid. A tall cupboard provides additional storage and organization space as it complements the woodwork throughout the kitchen. The sink is conveniently located behind the stovetop on an island for easy cooking and culinary tasks. Everything you need to prepare marvelous meals is in easy reach in this strategically arranged floor plan.

Traditional design meets contemporary color in this crisp, white kitchen with gray accents. Contrasts in color, surfaces, and textures form a visually stimulating view. Shiny floor tiles set on the diagonal add drama; solid surface countertops in cool gray frame the white stovetop and sink for pleasing contrasts. Cooking is easy with a microwave oven located right above the stovetop, with a conventional oven below.

1 The symmetrical vista of the sink includes decorative glass-paned wall cabinets with curving fan-shaped accents. Food preparation is a pleasure using this double bowl sink with a soap dispenser and hot water faucet for instant cups of tea or cocoa. The window is accented in light brown wood, forming a definitive frame from surrounding elements. Decorative cabinet hardware complements the interior design.

2 Here, cool white cabinets and ceiling complement icy gray hues in the countertop, floor, and walls. Smart cabinet design includes a wine rack next to the refrigerator. Glass-front wall cabinets encompass the corner niche of the kitchen, providing convenient and decorative storage of colorful ceramic bowls, glass bottles, and other kitchenware. Precision molding frames the ceiling soffit that provides gentle illumination from above. A seamless surface is achieved by using the same material for the countertop, the wall behind, and the underside of the upper cabinets.

1

2

This light, bright kitchen is inspired by the desert vistas of the Southwest with sandy colored floors, terracotta accent tiles, and cabinets in a complementary reddish-brown. The island has two distinct heights: the standard height housing a sink, and the higher section forming a beautiful dining counter for two. Open shelves permit easy storage of condiments, books, and culinary accessories. The tile work on the backsplash is decorative and functional with a terracotta border design along a white tile diamond pattern.

Striking granite countertops in mottled hues of browns, grays, and tans glisten atop cabinets and an island in this stunning kitchen. A wall of windows above the sink permits dazzling natural light throughout the space. A potted heather plant basks contentedly among primrose flowers atop the windowsill. An island cabinet in deep, rich, cherry adds a touch of class as it contrasts with the warm, light tones of the kitchen cabinets, window frames, and archway moldings. It comfortably seats four for informal dining and provides a unique conversational advantage having guests sit not beside, but across from each other. Two large archways create visual separation between the kitchen and the dining and seating areas. The floor plan is open and abundant with high ceilings and ample square footage. The rough surface of the floor tiles in natural stone contrast with shiny glass-like countertops, and complements the earth tone of the space.

INSET This archway vista is exquisitely framed in hardwood matching the kitchen cabinets and dining table in a spacious, open floor plan. A traditional chandelier complements the light brown hues of cabinets and table as it adds a warm glow to the room. A writing desk is conveniently positioned between two tall wall cabinets and below a large window, creating the perfect place to sort through mail, update the family calendar, or write one's next novel. High white ceilings, bright white walls, and light beige floor tiles encourage a spacious, open-air feeling.

1

2

1 White solid surface countertops stretch the length of the kitchen and cover the square island. Two sit comfortably at the island for convenient and informal dining. A few black accent tiles adorn the wall surface, producing contrast of color. Warm hardwood floors anchor the sea of white.

2 A solid surface countertop includes a built-in oval drain system, allowing for convenient drying of wet dishes. Black accent wall tiles complement the black stripe of color that adorns the front of the countertop and frames the sink.

3 Snow white cabinets, walls, and ceiling produce a dramatic monochromatic kitchen. The L-shaped design is a convenient floor plan for a kitchen this size, providing easy access to major appliances and numerous cabinets. Smooth surfaces and light, bright elements dominate for a clean, crisp design.

3

1

OPPOSITE: Delicate flowers and feathery leaves radiate from a center island as they decorate the floor with an intricate pattern. Decorative wall covering of a vintage embroidery pattern in red and blue complements the floral floor design of linoleum. Rich, wood cabinets are topped with shiny granite countertops of mottled brown, gray, and rust, providing lots of space for culinary tasks as well as decorative display.

1 Light brown cabinets in durable hardwood are complemented by gray countertops and stainless steel appliances. Neutral walls, ceiling, and floor materials produce a pleasing backdrop in complementary hues and textures. The unique cabinetry around the stove is framed by two ornate wooden corner details in the same luxurious hardwood as the cabinets. Beige ceramic wall tiles behind the stove add visual interest and complement color and texture. The rectangular framework of dark gray tiles separates two distinct sizes of beige tiles, the innermost pieces laid on the diagonal against a contrasting block formation.

2 A long, rectangular island contains a secondary stovetop and has plenty of counter space for food preparation. Preparing menus for large parties and holiday celebrations is a joy with two stoves, two wall ovens, stainless steel appliances, and lots of cooking space. The convex curved countertop can conveniently accommodate seating for two.

2

Bright blues and yellows pop within the cool country white of this kitchen. A huge basket of vivid yellow sunflowers and pale green hydrangeas bring in the beauty of the outdoors. Decorative and functional cabinet shelving surrounds the built-in eating nook, displaying a delightful array of delft earthenware dishes and canisters with other chinaware and books. Light, white curtains provide a soft backdrop and charming country ambiance.

INSET: A table nook provides the convenience of an eat-in kitchen with a table that accommodates three comfortably amidst this kitchen's cool, white backdrop. A still life of shiny bottles with fresh cut flowers in vibrant reds and yellows shares the spotlight with candlestick holders in various shades of blue. Rich hardwood floors anchor this pristine space.

A large, white sink framed in majestic blue tile dresses up a white countertop beautifully. Potted plants flourish beneath the windows and create a visual extension of the natural outdoor landscape. Any culinary task is a delight in this kitchen with inspirational vistas and creative configuration.

1 A stove is encompassed by an orderly symmetrical design of cabinets and framed by jars of dried herbs and spices in neat rows. A microwave and additional storage lies directly above. Kitchen organization is easy and neat with lots of cabinets, nooks, and crannies like these. Brass bars are attached to all of the countertops and match the cabinet hardware, providing handy places to hang dishtowels and oven mitts.

2 Cool white cabinets are complemented by icy blue accents in the wall tiles, floor tiles, and culinary accessories including delft earthenware. Sunlight streams in the window above the sink, and a deep windowsill easily accommodates elegant potted flowers and fresh herbs. The white walls are accented with blue borders matching the earthenware designs on display throughout the room.

Honey-hued cabinets are surrounded by neutral beige and white tones on the wall, ceiling and floor. A decorative stove hood is as ornately beautiful as it is functional, forming a handy shelf to display tin containers, candlesticks, and a ceramic pitcher. The Palladian window above the sink is sleek and contemporary, allowing natural sunlight to filter into the space. A round oak table and chairs adjacent to the kitchen complement the wood cabinets beautifully. Dining is cozy and cheerful in this country kitchen.

1 A charming round oak table seats four in the adjacent dining area. Built-in wall cabinets provide space to store table linens, silverware, and china conveniently next to the kitchen and in the dining area. Domed ceiling lights add a warm ambiance and enhance the cozy feeling of this country kitchen and dining area.

2 The stove is surrounded by multilevel storage units that hold condiments and cooking needs within easy reach. Lots of counter space makes food preparation a breeze. A stainless steel rack hangs behind the stove, providing a handy spot for necessities like salt, pepper, and a measuring cup. A small shelf extends from a rack that holds a jar of assorted wooden spoons and spatulas.

PREVIOUS: Color-washed cabinets in a striking Colonial blue-green create a homey feeling in this charming country kitchen. Contrasting floor tiles in earth tones are a pleasing addition to the other surfaces, textures, and colors in the room. Wall cabinets include a vintage-style plate rack where plates are displayed decoratively, yet are easy to reach. Beige and tan tiles cover the backsplash and produce a cohesive design statement with the matte, rough surface of the floor tiles. The island resembles a beautiful antique teacart, complete with open shelves and decorative spindles. **INSET:** Charm and function abound in this colorful kitchen. An ornate island like an antique teacart features a convenient stovetop and storage shelves. Culinary accoutrements and dried herbs hang gracefully from a pot rack that doubles as a shelf, supporting a basket and additional cooking implements. Lacey window treatments add a touch of romance and allow luminous sunlight to stream in.

1

2

1

1 This base cabinet houses a state-of-the-art wine cooler. The wall cabinet above provides storage for other culinary items and contains a wine rack for six bottles. Fetching cocktails is elegant and easy with this stunning cabinet design.

2 A pleasing contrast of colors, textures and surfaces adorns the angular design of this contemporary kitchen. Stainless steel appliances and stove hood are visually appealing amongst brown cabinets. Neutral floor tiles and ceiling form an elegant backdrop for rich hues and timeless nuances.

2

3 A professional-series stove and seating for three can be found in this functional island. Behind, a wall covering produces subtle contrast with rough texture and neutral color. Creatively framed wall art adds a touch of drama to the space with greenish-gray hues that complement the brushed stainless steel hood and mottled colors in the glistening granite. Dinner plates are beautifully displayed in the open-design dish rack beneath large cabinets with ample storage.

3

1 Symmetrical cabinet design forms an orderly environment. The large cabinet on the left is actually a refrigerator in disguise. Sparkling glass-front cabinet doors mirror the beauty of the kitchen and the tranquil scene outdoors.

2 This culinary haven features golden wood cabinets and a matching hardwood floor. A U-shaped design allows for easy and convenient food preparation, utilizing a minimum of steps from sink to stove to ovens. Rich granite countertops create lots of counter space; ample storage abounds in luxurious cabinets of varied heights with stylish moldings. A wall of windows provides an unobstructed view and fills the space with warm, inviting sunlight.

3 Walls of windows open to an exterior landscape of endless vistas. Open and airy, the high ceilings and light colored surfaces of this kitchen create a spacious, comfortable room. A raised countertop behind the stove provides seating with a spectacular view. This cooking space was designed for inspiration.

1

2

3

A combination of warm and cool neutral tones sets the stage for this contemporary kitchen. Smooth cabinet surfaces in cool gray complement the rough textures of the floor tiles. Chrome and stainless steel accents blend pleasingly within the space. Large windows behind the sink, glass doors that lead to the patio, and the skylight above all fill the kitchen with bright sunlight. The island is V-shaped with rounded edges to seat four. The opposite side of the island has sharp angular cuts to form a "V" between two cabinet storage spaces.

1 A contemporary range hood complements a cook top of transparent green glass. Wall tiles add an attractive muted pink and mauve element with unusual scalloped shapes. Elegant entertaining is easy in this contemporary kitchen full of modern conveniences.

2 The island is covered in a solid surface countertop that provides easy maintenance and durability. Four can dine comfortably while overlooking an inviting seating area in the room's corner.

3 In addition to providing seating for four and handy storage areas, the island also contains an oven. One can bake, prepare food, store items, and comfortably enjoy a meal all at one island.

Beige cabinets, neutral-colored floor tiles, and creative angles produce this marvelous contemporary kitchen. The island seating area includes shelves to display books and chinaware, as well as drawers to organize culinary supplies. A large picture window runs the length of the wall behind the sink, allowing breathtaking views of nature's landscape. Lush, green potted plants bring inside the feeling of the great outdoors.

1 A delightful desk is incorporated into the modern cabinet design, providing contemporary comfort for multitasking lifestyles. Counter-to-ceiling cabinets accentuate clean, orderly design elements and provide an abundance of storage space.

2 Festive, colored culinary accents and brightly hued food and flowers provide a joyous splash of color within this cool, white environment. The contemporary island is perfect for a romantic dinner for two, and also provides kitchen organization in ample drawers and cabinet space. The custom-made kitchen table is built with the solid surface countertop material, in a delightful and whimsical flower petal design.

3 Modern trends are manifested in this kitchen of clean lines and straight angles. Monochromatic splendor encompasses this space with accents in gray in the form of fine lines that border the cabinets, countertop, tabletop, appliances, and floor tiles. A vaulted ceiling above the dining area exaggerates the spacious appeal of the environment.

1

2

3

OPPOSITE: This kitchen is dominated by an open-air feeling with a multitude of outdoor landscape views. The upper wall cabinets suspended from the ceiling above the sink and countertop appear to float. The angular design of the island produces a circular floor plan with ample room within the space. Warm wood tones of the cabinets and neutral beige tones in the floor, ceiling, and countertops complement nature's beauty as seen through an endless wall of windows encompassing the entire length of the house. **INSET:** Hand-detailed custom cabinetry provides storage of culinary needs and countertop space for food preparation. A writer's desk is built into the base cabinets for additional convenience for the multitasking cook. The refrigerator and other major appliances appear to be cabinets themselves with the application of matching wood panels. Open and airy, this kitchen is a delightful place to entertain friends and family, or just linger with a cup of morning coffee.

1

1 The island not only provides seating for six, it houses the smooth surface cook top and provides additional storage space in the form of decorative shelves and drawers. Seating guests is not a problem in this luxurious kitchen. The counter to the left of the island is equipped with a built-in bar that seats four more. Adjacent to this, a dining table accommodates another six. Warm complementary colors and smooth surfaces and textures resonate comfort and coziness.

2 Exquisite wall cabinets hang suspended from the ceiling, both sides having transparent, paned doors that allow viewing straight through. Chinaware is conveniently stored here without cluttering the open ambiance.

2

1

A decorative tile insert on the floor coordinates with the backsplash wall tile to create a festive design in this angular kitchen. Warm wood cabinets complement the wood floor and contrast attractively with the countertop and tile elements.

1 An L-shaped cabinet configuration provides lots of workspace in this inviting kitchen. The countertop bar seats three for casual, no-fuss dining. Multilevel counters add visual interest and dining comfort.

2 A built-in desk provides additional working convenience in this kitchen. Plenty of counter space permits a writing area and storage of necessary books and stationery items.

2

1

2

1 Strong contrasts of dark and light surfaces create visual interest in this kitchen. Black and white polka-dot curtains add whimsy, and tie in the hues of the deep wood cabinets and the white solid surface countertop.

2 Black appliances produce a strong contrast with the neutral shades of the walls, ceiling, and floor in this kitchen. Medium brown cabinets contrast in color and texture with the countertops, walls, and appliances.

Neutral, beige cabinets and floor tiles blend into white walls and ceiling while charcoal-toned solid surface countertops contrast. High ceilings and an entire wall of windows enhance an open-air feeling.

1 A curved cabinet next to the dishwasher provides easy organization of oversized supplies like cookie trays, cutting boards, pizza stones, and other specialty pans, and hides them behind a sliding tambour door.

1

The island cabinet includes several drawers for kitchen organization. A shapely table jets out from the island forming a convenient peninsula where four can be seated comfortably. Decorative, diamond-shaped designs in the glass-front cabinets add a splendid touch of interest.

INSET: This wall consists of a row of true culinary convenience. Double wall ovens are next to a microwave oven and built-in television. A quaint roll-top desk provides additional comfort for multitaskers.

1

Drama and high-tech glitz fashion this stunning design. Every angle provides visual excitement with sleek, shiny surfaces and bold, stately colors. Luscious cherry cabinets are accented with diamonds of sparkling copper. Ceiling lights feature copper surfaces enhanced with white glass diamonds and hang from wood beams above, echoing the cabinets.

1 The large island is topped with a multi-hued granite in black, green, and gray. It also has an extended countertop surface large enough to seat two comfortably for an informal meal. The dishwasher is located right next to the sink for quick clean-up. The room is framed by contrasting cherry trim around windows set within warm beige walls.

2 This kitchen was inspired by the influences of Art Deco design. Vivid diamond accents flourish around the stove and adjacent cooking surface with swirling stainless steel. A hinged lid reveals a wok for preparing delicious and healthy stir-fry recipes with convenience and ease. The cabinet next to the stove has an authentic butcher-block top for the slicing and dicing of fruits and vegetables without the need of an additional cutting board.

2

1

2

Bright white cabinets, ceiling, and appliances contrast with an ebony granite countertop on an island that seats three behind a sleek stove-top. The island provides lots of storage space for organization of cookbooks and other tools of the trade.

1 Tranquil landscapes are visible through the Palladian-inspired window above the sink. Glorious moldings frame the window as if it were on display at an art gallery. Glistening sunlight filters into the snow-white interior accented with fresh flowers. Gleaming brass hardware accents white cabinets and a continuous brass bar surrounds the counters for a convenient place to hang dishtowels and oven mitts.

2 A row of cabinets behind the island includes a secondary sink, ample countertop space, and double wall ovens. The upper wall cabinets reveal a stunning collection of chinaware through clear glass panes. Three domed light fixtures of textured crystalline glass add additional illumination above the island.

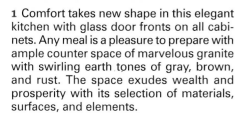

1 Comfort takes new shape in this elegant kitchen with glass door fronts on all cabinets. Any meal is a pleasure to prepare with ample counter space of marvelous granite with swirling earth tones of gray, brown, and rust. The space exudes wealth and prosperity with its selection of materials, surfaces, and elements.

2 A stainless steel refrigerator, stove, and hood complement natural organic hues in a granite countertop and backsplash. Wall cabinets extend to the ceiling, providing limitless storage space. Cooking is easy for everyone with these modern and elegant conveniences.

3 Easy living meets Euro style in this kitchen of shiny granite countertops and clean white cabinets. Three large windows frame the convenient double bowl sink, perfect for arranging cut flowers and preparing delicious meals. Open glass door panels enhance the airy look and create eye-catching storage areas. Stainless steel appliances complement the sleek elements of Euro style.

Warm earth tones of brown, beige, and tan surround this kitchen on the walls, ceiling, floor, countertops, and cabinets. Cozy and compact, this space has a welcoming and inviting design. Colors, textures, and surfaces harmonize. **INSET:** A convenient U-shaped design provides easy access to everything you need for quick and easy food preparation and clean-up afterwards. The organic shape of the countertop complements earthy colors and textures throughout the entire room.

1 Cool white hues of the walls, ceiling, cabinets, countertops, and appliances give this country-style kitchen a sparkling, updated look. The huge center island has a multitude of storage spaces as well as a countertop for ease of food preparation. There is a large double basin sink and a dishwasher in the island as well. Decorative and functional chinaware is displayed in the open shelves on the end of the island. Two can dine comfortably at this charming counter.

2 The wall cabinets above the sink are encased in two sides of paned glass that give a feeling of openness with a transparent view to the adjoining room. Stemware hangs neatly and conveniently under the cabinets, while a refrigerated wine cooler and a wine rack are located directly below, making bartending an easy task.

3 Beautiful oak floors anchor this vast vision of white cabinets, countertops, walls, and ceiling. A desk is conveniently built into the cabinets at the end of a long line of cabinets and appliances. The cabinet above the desk boasts lots of space to store stationery items and display chinaware and plants.

1

2

3

1

2

3

4

1 Light and bright walls, ceiling and floor create a pleasant backdrop for warm brown cabinets and floral window treatments. Beige countertops provide lots of space for food preparation and complement other neutral colors in the room. Several large windows and glass paned doors provide stimulating vistas of the great outdoors and create spaciousness. A dining table is conveniently located beyond the island for easy entertaining with a delightful view.

2 The triangular shape of this kitchen forms a very functional floor plan for food preparation, clean-up, and maintenance. The island seats two for casual meals and also contains the stovetop and storage areas for enhanced kitchen organization. The dishwasher and refrigerator have matching wood panels that appear as cabinets. Tambour siding panels elegantly hide two small appliance garages.

3 Stainless steel appliances, elegant wood cabinets, and glistening granite countertops merge to form a contemporary haven. High ceilings and beige walls and floor enhance a spacious feeling while the earth tone palette produces a cozy one.

4 An elegant desk is built into the corner of the room with luxurious granite countertops and an abundance of storage space. The desk adds contemporary convenience for planning the next week's meals or writing to a friend.

1

2

3

4

Contemporary drama exudes from this kitchen masterpiece. A distinct combination of angles, colors, textures, and surfaces combine to form an astounding modern environment filled with endless details of culinary delight. An angled ceiling of skylights permits limitless sunlight to dance and reflect upon state-of-the-art surfaces and materials. A picture window extends below the skylights, further enhancing the interior beauty with nature's glow. Contemporary cabinets in cool gray with lavender undertones are complemented by Italian marble floor tiles made of swirling hues of rust, chestnut, and chocolate brown.

1 A small corner cabinet neatly stores wine with modern, dramatic flair.

2 The refrigerator, blending in seamlessly with the wall cabinets and perpetuating the neat, orderly façade of this modern design.

3 Sleek, modern cabinets cradle a built-in television for state-of-the-art viewing convenience.

4 Glistening glass blocks form an intriguing window behind the sink. A symmetrical vista of an island with the sink and cabinets behind creates order and stability within the room. A visual feast abounds with the combination of geometric shapes and organic surfaces. High ceilings intensify an envied openness.

1

2

3

1 A long row of light taupe cabinets is complemented by neutral walls, ceiling, and floor tiles. Accent wall tiles in various shades of blue add a touch of whimsy to this updated, country-inspired design. Lots of counter space provides easy food preparation for large and small gatherings of friends and family.

2 This row of custom cabinets includes double wall ovens, a refrigerator, and lots of storage space for all culinary needs. Convenient countertop surfaces at either end provide easy food preparation.

3 Base and wall cabinets feature a decorative design element with open corner shelves that display cherished chinaware and luscious potted plants with variegated leaves and blossoms. White solid surface countertops produce a subtle contrast with the light cabinets.

Contemporary country charm produces an inviting kitchen. The repetition of circular shapes in the arched doorway, kitchen nooks, and window designs creates a unique and unusual look. A field of muted red, white, and gray tones in the floor tiles, brick wall structures, and granite countertops create a pleasing backdrop for warm, white cabinets and cool, white walls. Arched ceiling coves and brick wall accents turn this kitchen into a romantic Parisian bistro. A tall wall cabinet is complemented by an arched ceiling cove and decorative framing of multi-toned bricks. Organic plants and a whimsical soft sculpture of a waiter add additional charm.

A sea of elegant, custom cherry cabinets is anchored by oak hardwood floors, producing a stunning design statement in this expansive kitchen. Neutral hues of walls and ceiling balance the concentration of dark, rich colors in the space. The island contains lots of workspace, a sink and stovetop, shelves for books and chinaware, and numerous drawers for storage. The large picture window above the primary sink accentuates the airy atmosphere of this ultra-spacious environment.

INSET: Any cook would be thrilled to work in this kitchen with a refrigerator, double ovens, and an island sink and stovetop all within close reach. Elegant surfaces and textures just add to the overall appeal. Shiny ebony granite creates a polished, dramatic look that boasts easy maintenance. The counter extends for dining space on the island with the addition of a few comfy chairs, or it can serve as a very spacious food preparation area, as shown.

Luxurious cherry cabinets are beautifully handcrafted with fine decorative details and complementary brass hardware. The multilevel surfaces of the island are elegant, and the shelves provide easy storage of cookbooks and decorative chinaware. Exquisite bas-relief images decorate the tiled walls with monochromatic tones providing contrast with dark surrounding surfaces of cabinets and countertops.

The professional stove is topped with a beautifully decorative and functional hood with bas-relief carvings that complement floral accent tiles on the wall. Country charm continues with the wall cabinet adjacent to the stove. Dishes are nicely displayed in the open-design plate rack that provides visual interest and working convenience.

INSET: An elegant niche is built into the cabinets, providing a decorative cove to display cherished chinaware and collectibles. Two lights illuminate the items within the space and an ornate acroterium adorns the top in a leaf motif.

OPPOSITE: Extremely high ceilings, an entire wall of windows, and neutral earth tones create a kitchen that feels spacious and open. Traditional charm is exemplified in custom cabinetry and decorative details throughout the room. The windows have an interesting mirrored effect with a coffered ceiling. A delicate floral print adorns the walls. Taupe and tan floor tiles complement the light, washed color of the cabinets and matching tile backsplash.

INSET: Mottled green, ebony, beige, and taupe commingle in the granite countertop. The hyoid shape of the floor plan provides comfort while preparing meals for two or for many. The refrigerator appears as another cabinet with matching wood surface panels and hardware.

This modest-sized kitchen is bountiful with country charm and fine, handcrafted details. Knotted pine cabinets in shades of honey create a warm and welcoming perimeter. Beige walls and ceiling complement the color scheme and make the kitchen appear more spacious. Hardwood floors have a terracotta tile accent that adds decorative interest and functionality to the workstation at the sink.

1 Exquisite, hand-crafted cabinet details are present throughout this kitchen. This detail shows wooden slide out shelves for convenient storage of pots and pans in the cabinet next to the stove.

2 The refrigerator appears to be a continuation of the cabinets with matching pine wood panels that completely encase the appliance. Floor-to-ceiling cabinets provide ample storage of groceries, and a wine rack stores a large selection of favored vintage bottles.

3 The cabinet next to the refrigerator is custom-fitted with door shelves to hold a multitude of condiments, herbs, and spices.

1

2

3

1

2

3

The countertop is accented with a built-in cutting surface of delightfully decorative tiles that match the backsplash around the entire kitchen. The countertop also provides a seating area for quick and convenient meals. Some details are not meant to be prominent in the room, such as the stove hood that inconspicuously hangs between two wall cabinets.

1 Every inch of space has been used to full capacity in this kitchen. The sink base has a wonderful foldout drawer to store a selection of sponges, brushes, and other cleaning tools. The double bowl sink makes food preparation and clean up easy. The contiguous shades of beige on and around the counter are exemplified by the matching hue of the sink.

2 Glistening crystal stemware dangles above a built-in wine rack, creating convenient storage as well as a pleasing visual design.

3 The cutlery drawer is equipped with elegant matching inserts that provide neat and convenient separation for knives, forks, and spoons.

The kitchen counter design provides casual dining for four. An adjacent family room enlivens the space with vibrant reds, yellows, and turquoise hues. Turquoises and yellows are evident in the kitchen with decorative chinaware and a matching window shade, tying the two rooms together with subtle color complements.

1 In addition to conventional burners, the stovetop is equipped with a built-in grill. Healthy, tasty meals can have the flavor of outdoor grilling year-round, without leaving the convenience and comfort of the kitchen for a snow-covered deck or rainy patio.

2 These modern cabinets are equipped with the latest technical advances. Sliding shelves pull out for an enhanced food storage experience. A decorative collection of copper culinary accoutrements adorns the top of the cabinets.

3 The distinct contrast of black and white is the focal point of this kitchen. Contemporary white cabinets are topped with charcoal gray countertops, while cathedral ceilings and a skylight make the space feel larger than it is. The diamond pattern on the floor adds a touch of whimsy.

2

1

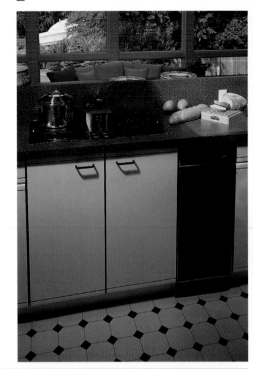

3

Contemporary drama excites the senses in this streamlined design in white. Smooth surfaces, curved walls, and contrasting textures invigorate the room. Sparkling natural light dances freely in this kitchen through several windows, skylights, and a curving wall of transparent glass block. White solid surface countertops have a contrasting ebony edge that complements a black floor. Cooking space curves around the room and extends seamlessly to dining space for family and guests.

INSET: Bright white appliances, cabinets, countertops, walls, and ceiling form an endless sea of white. Bright primary and secondary hues of food and culinary accents are the only splash of color in this monochromatic world of culinary comfort.

A continuous wall of cabinets surrounds this spacious kitchen, providing endless storage space and organizational potential. Some of the cabinets have glass-front doors that allow picturesque views of cherished heirlooms and accents. A still life of baskets, plants, china, and earthenware above the wall cabinets adds charm and beauty. **INSET:** Cozy elegance abounds in this home, with comfy furniture of charming plaid fabrics surrounding a romantic, crackling fireplace. Vaulted ceilings and an open floor plan create a spectacular view of the gourmet kitchen. Pink, mauve, and beige fabric tones and family room elements complement the pleasing shades of wood in the adjacent kitchen, like the matching fireplace hearth and kitchen cabinets.

OPPOSITE: Curved angles produce movement and visual delight in the kitchen and adjacent dining room. Al fresco enchantment is brought indoors with vaulted ceilings above the dining table, resembling an outdoor gazebo with its exquisitely executed skylights encased in blond wood. The curved exterior wall is made of floor-to-ceiling windows providing gorgeous outdoor views in this interior gazebo design. An island comprises the sink, dishwasher, storage cabinets, and a unique, two-level countertop; the lower a mauve solid surface, and the upper a matching mauve tile. **INSET:** A convenient storage space for cleaning tools is located directly under the sink in a tiny, pull-out door, so that no space is wasted. A daisy and iris arrangement in pink, white, and purple with decorative greens and heather sprigs rests in a silver ice bucket.

1

2

3

1 Beige floor tiles, white walls, and white ceilings are the neutral palette surrounding rich, deep wood in this traditional kitchen. Creative angles enhance the ample square footage in this floor plan. All major appliances are in close proximity of each other in a handy triangular design that ensures working convenience to the chef. A long line of countertop extends the entire perimeter of the kitchen, transforming from cooking to dining space, with seating for three. A delicate balance of color and texture contrasts blends effortlessly to create this comfortable and cohesive look.

2 Seemingly endless cabinets and countertops provide a multitude of storage space and room for food preparation within an opulent, yet comfortable design. The center island contributes to spatial movement with a delicate curve that supplies additional storage, lots of counter space, and a secondary sink. Cooking a romantic meal for two or for a large party is equally easy in this professionally appointed kitchen.

3 Perfect for writing letters or reading a cookbook, this built-in desk cabinet adds charm and elegance with multitasking convenience. It features nooks and crannies of various sizes and shapes to display favorite heirlooms and treasures along with storage for stationery supplies.

Deep, rich color and smooth, shiny surfaces blend seamlessly in this dramatic room. Glistening ebony granite caresses luxurious brown cabinets in a complementary fashion. Textured taupe wall coverings create an interesting contrast with smooth surfaces of the cabinets, countertop, and hardwood floor. Entertaining is easy in this finely appointed culinary retreat.

1 Earth tones blend warmly in this large, workable environment. Beautiful natural lighting fills the space as it shines through a large window above the sink. The shelf above the sink is decorated with a delightful array of culinary tools and green plants. The long, rectangular floor plan provides an abundance of elegant workspaces, including a completely appointed bar.

2 The luxurious bar is equipped with a wine cooler, sink, and lots of handy countertop space in durable and easy-to-maintain ebony granite. Sparkling glassware rests elegantly behind a wall of transparent glass doors for easy access. Cocktails for two or twenty are effortless to make here.

1

2

This view of the center island shows a secondary sink conveniently located next to a wine cooler. An expansive granite countertop makes ample room for food preparation and is equipped with a stovetop range. A multitude of storage space accommodates cooking equipment right where you need it most.

1 Cranberry walls catapult an otherwise subdued color scheme into a world of vibrancy and excitement. At the island, three distinct heights of countertop provide a visual feast of decorative displays. Crimson Gerber daisies burst into bloom from a shiny copper planter, while lit candles add a touch of romance. Festive place settings wait for invited guests, and a luscious cake waits to be served in style.

2 Country charm with a splash of elegance describes this unique and luxurious kitchen. Cinnamon-colored cabinets and hardwood floors create a warm, inviting, and spacious room. An eclectic collection of accents including sparkling crystal, bone china, a copper planter, romantic candles, fresh flowers, and whimsical sculptures solidifies a cozy, at-home feeling.

1

Warm wood tones are complemented by deep red wall accents and white ceilings. The slight curve of the kitchen wall leads cohesively to a dining room table, and a continuation of the red kitchen wall engulfs the dining room walls also. A charming accent wall covered in a country red plaid design creates overall ambiance.

OPPOSITE: A professional stove is elegantly surrounded by medium-toned cabinets and shiny, sleek granite. Mottled granite complements the design with a combination of light and dark tones including ebony, cinnamon, taupe, and moss green. Cooking and baking is an effortless task with a multiple-burner stove and two ovens. The stove hood is completely camouflaged by cabinets that help to form a cohesive and symmetrical wall. Fine, hand-carved brackets contrast with the white wall behind the stove, and produce an elegant visual frame on either side of the stove.

1 Traditional design is brought to life with earthy wood tones and shiny granite. Some of the cabinets have beautifully executed bas-relief scroll details. The island invites elegant dining for three and has open shelves for storage and display.

2 A vintage-style sink basin provides convenient use and easy maintenance with large, deep dimensions. Cooking is a joy in a kitchen of custom cabinets, elegant granite counter-tops, and inviting earth tones throughout. High ceilings and large windows complete a large, comfortable room.

Glossy granite countertops wind all the way around the kitchen and include a spacious desk perfect for reading a favorite magazine or taking notes while trying a new recipe. Sunny yellow walls make a bright and happy room and complement the earth tones present in the various surfaces and textures. A mosaic design in the linoleum floor creates a permanent rug pattern with complementary blue, brown, beige, and tan colors.

INSET: This close-up view shows the complex detail in a linoleum floor design, as well as the inspired paintings on a chair with tree limbs as the footrest and main support. Chestnut and beige floor tiles complement the matching hues of the cabinets throughout the kitchen. Creativity, artistic vision, and masterful execution of fine surfaces and textures transform this kitchen into a feast for the senses.

OPPOSITE: The rustic outdoors inspired this unique kitchen, with country accents and welcoming ambiance. Tree limbs were artistically transformed into whimsical chairs with festive foliage paintings and bright-hued borders in a rainbow of colors. The diamond-patterned floor is masterfully made of natural linoleum. An exquisite border like a tile mosaic surrounds the long island. The island has seating for four, a large double bowl sink, lots of countertop space, and ample storage in numerous cabinets. Pale shades of yellow caress the walls and ceiling as if kissed by continual sunlight in an everlasting day. Nature's outdoor atmosphere is alive with warmth and serenity in this expansive kitchen of creative ingenuity.

Contemporary glitz engulfs this huge kitchen of dramatic details in surfaces, textures, and materials. Glossy granite countertops glide along the expansive row of cabinets with endless space for a multitude of tasks. Natural attraction tantalizes the senses as countless windowpanes paint exquisite outdoor scenes, bringing in the beauty of the lush outdoors. The island is covered in rich granite and provides elegant dining for two. A secondary sink and ample storage areas in several drawers and cabinet space are also part of the island. Off-white floor tiles mirror the neutral ceiling, creating an added feeling of spaciousness and freedom. Mundane meals are not on the menu in this extravagant culinary haven.

INSET: This kitchen comes complete with a state-of-the-art professional series stove. Numerous burners and two ovens make cooking for a crowd easy. Stainless steel appliances complement the blond cabinets and surrounding neutral hues. Long expanses of countertop on either side of the stove provide lots of space for food preparation.

1

1 The refrigerator is encased in floor-to-ceiling cabinetry, providing ample storage and kitchen organization. Tall shelves adorn the end of this wall of cabinets with enticing groupings of chinaware and books. High ceilings and pale color values create a light and airy environment, perfect for comfortable entertaining.

2 Lush green leaves and vibrant red peppers flourish on a potted plant as it drinks in nourishing sunlight through windowpanes overlooking a spectacular view. Highly polished ebony granite contrasts in color and texture with the beautiful light hue of wood cabinets.

3 A built-in cupboard extends from the floor to the ceiling in dramatic ebony with textured glass door panels that complement dramatic ambiance and contrasts with neutral colors. Three elegant place settings wait at the countertop peninsula. Streamlined light fixtures of polished steel and glass enhance the existing light above the counter and island areas.

2

3

1 Warm, inviting shades of beige and white produce serenity in this delicious kitchen. A large, rectangular skylight allows sunlight to stream in and illuminate the room with sparkling luster. Three windows at the sink add additional natural light to this bright, open, and airy environment. There is no contrast with the refrigerator, dishwasher, and stove hood, as they blend in with the colors and materials of the cabinets that surround them. Lots of countertop space makes culinary tasks easy to handle.

2 An elegant hood above the stove matches the cabinets and complements the neutral hues encompassing the room. Bright, white wall tiles blend seamlessly with the smooth white countertops. Clear glass-front doors of the wall cabinets expose beautiful still-life groupings of fine china, glistening crystal, and heirloom silver.

3 Nature's beauty is seen through three large windows at the sink that provide pleasing natural light as well as dreamy vistas of the delightful landscape. This kitchen is equipped with many modern conveniences, including a pullout cutting board next to the sink. Food preparation is a joy with these kinds of design extras.

1

2

3

1 Culinary conveniences lie at every turn in this well-appointed kitchen. Two wall ovens have ample countertop space on either side to set down that hot pan right when it emerges, and the microwave oven is only a step away, too. A multitude of cabinets provides ample storage for numerous culinary tools and food supplies. A large drawer beneath the ovens holds all necessary pots and pans.

2 Complementary colors, surfaces, and textures creates cohesiveness in this kitchen. The solid surface countertop material also forms the sink. The white faucet and accessories are the final touch to this monochromatic blend.

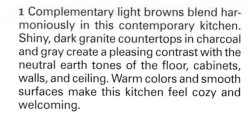

1

1 Complementary light browns blend harmoniously in this contemporary kitchen. Shiny, dark granite countertops in charcoal and gray create a pleasing contrast with the neutral earth tones of the floor, cabinets, walls, and ceiling. Warm colors and smooth surfaces make this kitchen feel cozy and welcoming.

2 The stainless steel refrigerator, dishwasher, and sink complement the sleek, clean lines in this modern environment. Spacious enough to organize a multitude of culinary needs, this kitchen also has a handy layout that makes culinary tasks easy to accomplish.

2

1 Top-of-the-line custom cabinets and rich, luxurious materials comprise this extravagant kitchen with a visually stimulating design. The crescent-shaped island boasts elegant dining for four atop a gorgeous granite countertop in an array of mottled earth tones. A beautiful end cabinet has three shelves to display favorite cookbooks and treasures. Very tall ceilings and light beige hues exaggerate the already open and delightfully airy ambiance of this room.

2 This kitchen is fully equipped with state-of-the-art appliances, including a professional series stove. The beige tiled wall behind the stove is complementary in color and texture to the rest of the kitchen, simultaneously providing a delicate and pleasing pattern with small contrasting tiles in gray. In addition to the storage cabinets and seating space, the island has a built-in wine rack to hold several bottles of a favorite vintage. The sink is also located in the island, making it a convenient focal point at the center of the room.

1

2

3

1 This contemporary kitchen has a formidable, straight-forward design with modern conveniences that any chef would love. Bold, stainless steel appliances complement milky white cabinets, ceiling, and walls. Royal blue wall tiles accent the white tones, and strong, vivid colors of blue, red, yellow and green catch the eye in pleasing culinary items and decorative accessories.

2 This detail shows a custom drawer that holds flour and other dry ingredients conveniently at the peninsula workspace. This makes preparing a favorite pie dough a breeze with all ingredients in easy reach. A dark marble top is handy for rolling out pale dough, and contrasts in color and texture with surrounding surfaces.

3 Vibrant flowers of yellow, pink, red, and orange are arranged in a brilliant pitcher at the secondary sink in this large, contemporary kitchen. The stainless steel sink complements a clean white color palette and matches detail elements like stylish drawer pulls.

1 This island perpetuates the sea of white elegance with coordinating cabinets, countertop, and chairs. The stovetop has two tile inserts on either side, nestled in the countertop to act as built-in heat-resistant surfaces for a hot pan. These tiles coordinate with the royal blue tiles on the wall behind.

2 Continuity of design is evident in this view of the kitchen, with a series of rectangular shapes incorporating a delightfully modern environment. There are two prominent bookshelves, a stone accent wall, long island, peninsula workstation, a wall of cabinets, two windows, and doorways that all make a strong rectangular statement. Natural earth tones and rough textures of the stone wall contrasts with other smooth, monochromatic surfaces. High ceilings and an open floor plan make this kitchen feel very spacious indeed.

1

2

3

3 A handy floor layout in a triangular design encompassing the stove, sink, and refrigerator makes a perfectly efficient workspace out of this large kitchen. Even though the kitchen is spacious, one does not have to walk far to have all the necessary items handy to prepare meals. A unique spice rack that spins for quick viewing of all available items is attached to the wall; no more rummaging around in a cabinet overflowing with toppling, unorganized bottles of herbs.

1

2

Highly lacquered beige cabinets surround this kitchen with gleaming beauty and function. Long stretches of solid surface countertops provide ample workspace with an easy-to-maintain material in a complementary off-white hue. The stove is conveniently located at the point of a triangular design, with countertops and cabinets on either side for storage and food preparation.

1 A fine conglomeration of man-made materials, natural wood, and glass surfaces join forces to present a kitchen with fascinating elements and a space-age design. Round, curving lines of the island boldly incorporate a stainless steel sink in a complementary oval shape. Symmetrical light fixtures have an extraterrestrial flair in the shape of flying saucers and made of glass and shiny brass accents. Complementary surfaces in beige and brown produce warmth while stainless steel and glass add a touch of cool, contemporary contrast.

2 Stainless steel wall coverings add polished elegance to this modern design. Sandwiched between two base cabinets is a handy wine cooler to store a variety of favorite vintages. Fine details and shiny surfaces inspire the culinary creativity of chefs and guests alike in this enticing kitchen.

Spacious elegance abounds in this Tuscan-inspired kitchen with an open floor plan and cathedral ceilings of bright white. Custom, handmade cabinets create an inviting feeling in light brown with a delicate white-washed effect. The large island has a contrasting countertop of glossy granite in a variety of earth tones. The other cabinets have a solid surface countertop in bright white that creates visual continuity with the colors of the ceiling and walls. Shiny copper accoutrements surround the kitchen with visual delight and the lush, vibrant greenery adds a welcoming touch of the outdoors. Beautiful tiles cover the floor in matte beige tones that enhance the overall beauty of the design.

1 An arched window above the sink is both decorative and functional. Built-in blinds conveniently direct glistening sunlight as needed. Hand-stenciled grape vines adorn the top of the window in pleasingly muted shades that complement the interior color scheme and enhance a Tuscan ambiance. The sea of white is continuous on the countertop with a matching white sink.

2 Decorative wall tiles add a festive touch to the kitchen with terracotta hues that complement the cabinets. Small white tiles in the mosaic unify the surrounding white tones of the wall, countertop, and accessories. Transparent glass doors on the wall cabinet reveal still-life images of fine china. Bright, summery flowers decorate the room with vibrant color.

1

2

Warm beige cabinets and floor tiles are complemented by white countertops and appliances in this quaint kitchen. The modest island seats two for casual meals and provides storage space for kitchen organization. Decorative touches in wood and wicker accessories add a feeling of warmth to this kitchen, and deeply hued china creates visual sparks of color throughout. A display of delightful dishes, cups and saucers rests contentedly on top of the built-in rack that runs the length of the wall.

INSET: Romantic charm is achieved through soft, creative lighting in this kitchen. Lace cutouts in the delicate fabric window treatments add a feminine touch. Fresh flowers and plants are natural choices to complete a most welcoming ambiance in this pretty room.

Subdued gray hues embellish an extraordinary kitchen with top-of-the-line surfaces, materials, and appliances. Luxurious oak floors bring warmth and comfort to the room. Granite countertops glisten in cool gray shades with dark and light veins. Large windows surround the sink along three walls for a panoramic landscape view. Three amber light fixtures dangle above the L-shaped island, providing warm accent lighting. Stainless steel accents including the range hood and sink complement cool tones. The dishwasher is nearly invisible next to the sink with its individual pullout drawers that look like ordinary cabinets. Detailed accents such as hand-carved scrolls embellishing corner walls add a special touch.

INSET: This kitchen is packed with smart design elements. The stove has a handy water faucet for filling pots directly from the wall behind it. The island has a beautiful glass-front cabinet that stores stemware elegantly. Romantic meals for two can be eaten at the island with a wonderful landscape view through the kitchen windows. The refrigerator looks like additional cabinets with matching wood panels that cover the surface.

Glorious sunlight shines into this kitchen from every possible angle. Countless windowpanes open this kitchen and adjoining dining room to the tranquil essence of lustrous natural beauty. A granite-laden rectangular island takes center stage; pristine white cabinets and woodwork surround both rooms, creating a retreat for the inspired cook or houseguest. Lustrous, dark brown butcher-block covers the rest of the kitchen cabinets, complementing an ebony wood floor and contrasting with the many crisp white surfaces.

White ceramic tiles cover the stove hood and backsplash here, perpetuating a visual sea of bright white. Conveniently located, the island serves as the perfect workstation for preparing everything from a holiday turkey to batches of delicious cookies. Storage space is abundant, making kitchen organization easy to achieve.

1 Beautiful glass-front cabinets around the stove store a variety of cooking staples including pastas, teas, and spices, all in handy reach of the stove, making cooking easy and storage lovely with an assortment of clear glass containers.

2 These corner cabinets make a bold statement in white as they bend to form a visually pleasing curve around the room. Everyday glassware as well as crystal stemware is conveniently stored here for easy access. Handcrafted molding adorns the tops of the cabinets and encircles the entire kitchen in detailed elegance.

1

2

The entire kitchen is surrounded with transparent windowed cabinets that permits sunlight to pass right through, creating an astoundingly open and visually exciting effect. These cabinets are chock-full of white china and stoneware with the occasional vibrant color or hued trim. This kitchen exudes that summery, cottage-by-the-sea feeling with crisp white surfaces and enchanting window vistas. Entertaining is a breeze in this wonderfully appointed kitchen with professional series appliances.

INSET: This detail shows the beautiful workmanship of custom cabinets. A multitude of kitchenware is lovingly displayed behind clear glass panes, creating stunning still-life images.

Uniquely captivating, a balance of function, style, and comfort welcomes you into this extraordinary kitchen. Variegated wood cabinets are topped with solid surface white countertops and glossy granite on an island. Light neutral hues of the ceiling, walls, and floor tiles make a tranquil backdrop. An elongated island includes a secondary sink, stovetop, and numerous cabinets for storage, many equipped with built-in shelves that pull out for easy pot and pan storage.

Double wall ovens are creatively incorporated into a corner cabinet. Floor-to-ceiling cabinets provide endless space; even the family dog has a special place in the kitchen with a built-in bed within the base cabinet, while canine-inspired wood molding depicts cutouts in the shapes of bones, adding a touch of whimsy.

1 A deep cabinet above the oven has partitions to hold large serving trays, platters, and other baking sheets that are usually a challenge to store.

2 Family planning is easy at this beautiful built-in desk that ends a long row of inspired cabinet design. White countertops made of a solid surface material provide a great writing surface at the desk, and are perfect for food prep and easy maintenance in the rest of the kitchen. Variegated wood cabinets are complemented by neutral surroundings in this open space.

Decked out with two refrigerators, this is a gourmet's delight for food preparation and culinary creativity. Every modern convenience is at one's fingertips. The serene color scheme of the sea flows from the kitchen into the family room. Tropical plants, a large aquarium, and a cozy leather sofa in a delicious shade of aquamarine transform this room into an underwater oasis.

1 Inspired by the beauty of the ocean, contemporary comfort embraces this seaside kitchen with stylish cabinets, appliances, and accoutrements. An entire wall of windows separates the kitchen from the outdoor porch for endless hours of natural sunlight and exquisite landscape views from any perch. Tropical delights are enjoyed year round with this ingenious design that supports green living.

2 Dark, turquoise ceramic tiles float across the floor in a tranquil seashore fashion for a soothing backdrop for beige and white kitchen elements. A hushed shade of turquoise covers the walls and ceiling, creating a subliminal vision of an underwater retreat interpreted for a practical kitchen. The island has ample storage space, a sink, and casual dining for two.

The Palladian-inspired window above the sink majestically reveals a fantastic view of nature's landscape. The large center island includes a state-of-the-art stovetop with six burners, storage for a multitude of culinary accoutrements, and elegant dining for three. Bright white tones blend from one surface to the next with clean, contemporary flair.

1 Contemporary elegance abounds in this monochromatic palette of white on white. Clean, elegant lines form a functional and modern kitchen design with lots of storage space and a large expanse of countertop. The gray mottled granite on the island contrasts with white solid surface countertops used throughout the rest of the kitchen. The attention to detail in this kitchen is impeccable. Brass hardware adorns various elements, including drawer and door handles, the secondary sink, light fixtures above the island, and the counter rail that extends around the whole kitchen.

2 Casual meals are easily prepared and eaten conveniently at this kitchen's functional island. Three can dine in comfort with a wonderful view of the adjoining family room through elegant arches with columns. White tones reach out into the family room as well, with a gorgeous fireplace surrounded by textured stone in nature's finest blend of beige, taupe, and gray. A blazing fire in the hearth and lit candles on the mantle ensure cozy, romantic ambiance in this wonderful home.

Ultra-stylish elements of the finest materials and surfaces create this luxurious Art Deco kitchen. Defined lines and geometric shapes intensify the theme. Exquisite hardwood floors in honey maple feature diamond inlays that mirror the hardware on the cabinets. Ebony and white speckled marble covers the cabinets, island, and backsplash walls. An intricate, coffered ceiling creates visual interest overhead in shades of white in the Deco shape of the chandelier. The refrigerator, dishwasher, and trash compactor melt into the cabinets with wood panels. A striking staircase in rich cherry ascends to the second floor with elegance.

INSET: Graduated heights of cabinets form an intriguing wall behind the sink, providing a series of pedestals to display assorted sculptures and decorative accent pieces. This element opens up the space to a spectacular view of two huge picture windows with numerous panes in a rectangular frame. This kitchen is a bountiful harvest of culinary luxury that is a feast for the eyes as well as the appetite.

Vibrant red walls provide exuberant color in this kitchen and dining room. The large picture window opens up to a lush landscape in contrasting colors and textures. The triangular-shaped island is a treasure trove; two can dine in elegant comfort, numerous cabinets provide ample storage space, a secondary sink adds ease in cooking tasks, and a secondary dishwasher ensures stress-free cleanup. Stainless steel sinks and stovetop complement the polished marble surfaces that surround them. All of these combined elements of color, texture, and materials create visual continuity in this Deco-inspired design.

INSET: Attention to detail can be appreciated with this close-up of the sink and cabinets. An intricate inlaid wood design embellishes the cabinet doors for a radiance of its own. The multileveled structure behind the sink is expertly executed in light and dark woods with perfect details. Diamond-shaped bronze hardware completes the design with just the right amount of dazzle to remain subtle and full of class.

ABOUT THE AUTHOR

Oleta Neith is a writer specializing in books about design. She has decades of experience as a photo stylist for architectural interior photography as well as product photography, and is responsible for most of the styling and all of the photo assisting in this book. Jack D. Neith is a professional interior photographer with over 25 years of experience. His work can be found on covers and in annual reports, product brochures, and advertisements internationally. Other Schiffer books written by Jack D. and Oleta Neith include *Power Rooms*.